To Gerty —
    hope you recognize
some of these people
and feel i've done
honor to them —
    as i honor you
    my sister

        Anne

December 2004

AN IMPERFECT LOVER

Poems and Watercolors by Georgianna Orsini

AN IMPERFECT LOVER

Poems and Watercolors by Georgianna Orsini

CavanKerry ◊ Press LTD.

Library of Congress Cataloging-in-Publication Data
Orsini, Georgianna, 1932-
   An imperfect lover : poems / by Georgianna Orsini.
      p. cm.
   ISBN 0-9707186-7-5
   I. Title.
   PS3615.R66147 2004
   811'.6--dc21

                                      2003046048

Cover illustration and portrait of the author: Georgianna Orsini
Copyright: Georgianna Orsini, New York.
Cover and book design by Peter Cusack.

First Edition

Printed in the United States of America

CavanKerry Press Ltd.
Fort Lee, New Jersey
www.cavankerrypress.com

CavanKerry Press is grateful to the National Endowment for the Arts
and the New Jersey State Council on the Arts
for its support of this book.

ACKNOWLEDGMENTS

Grateful acknowledgment is made to the literary journals in which the following poems, sometimes in earlier versions, were published.

Boulevard: "The Perfect Lover"
Worcester Review: "Closing a Door", "A Complaint"
The Texas Review: "Tomato Sandwiches"
The Islander, Sanibel: "Canoeing, In Concert"
The Evening Reader: "Hypocritic Oath"

I am always grateful for the delight and knowledge given to me by my poetry teachers Bob Phillips, Colette Inez, and Babette Deutsch; my painting teachers Hanne Boonstra and Joyous Miller; my piano teachers Lilly Trog-Prinz and Judith Burganger; and, not least, Kenton Coe, composer-collaborator, and Anne Smith, fellow artist conspirator.

To Armando: "Where are you?" I ask.
"Here," you always answer.

To Molly: Who made me Take Heart

Table of Contents

Foreword

One is hard put to summon to mind a poet who also is adept in the graphic arts. There are Michelangelo, Blake, Rossetti, Cocteau, perhaps Branwell Brontë, Denton Welch, e.e. cummings, and of course Beatrix Potter. It is Potter of whom Georgianna Orsini reminds me. Not her writing, of course, which takes on a fierceness never found in Peter Rabbit or Benjamin Bunny, but her paintings. Even Orsini's titles are whimsical (*Drawing of Mice in Spoon, Drawing of Shoes with Figures Inside*, etc.). And all is not whimsy certainly. One has to be impressed by her wonderful owl in *Drawing with Owl and Cow* and the *Heart Woman*. In such a picture the aural and the visual coalesce—the sounds of *owl* and *cow*, the fancy of a heart woman who confesses to having the heart of a lover, and that owl, who asks, "who are you, who am I?" The owl is worthy of comparison with Charles Burchfield's *Arctic Owl and Winter Moon* (1960). There are owls elsewhere in Orsini's pictures as well. Traditionally owls, in their different varieties, appear to humans as wise, patient, introspective, brooding, and able to see in the dark—qualities of the intuitive artist as well. Orsini's owl is an artist-figure.

Orsini's *Drawing with Owl and Cow* is a picture that asks fundamental questions about human existence. Samuel Johnson said a book should help us either enjoy life or endure it. I'd say Orsini's book does both, with enjoyment (especially in the pictures) and endurance coexisting like the tastes in a sweet and sour sauce. Orsini would enjoy the comparison, I think, since in addition to her writing and painting, she is a gourmet cook (and a pianist, and a gardener, and the list goes on). I think it is fine that CavanKerry Press has had the vision to bring together two of her arts in one volume.

"The Heart Makes a Will" is a strong poem beginning a strong book. It has the toughness of Sylvia Plath and Anne Sexton, two poets to whom I would compare Orsini. At one point she even likens herself to roadkill! But she is more Sexton than Plath. What saved many of Sexton's poems from bathos was her sense of humor. (Nobody ever died laughing at Plath.) Orsini has fun telling us mice are "a snap to catch." One can just hear that mouse trap snapping. Then there is her cunning slant-rhyme of *falsetto* and *fellatio*. There is a control in these poems that is admirable. The two Stop signs in *Drawing with Owl and Cow* cannot be ignored. The poet is telling us we have to curb our emotions. In the poem "The Heart Makes a Will," Orsini compares the heart in love to "a silly thing, / much like a chicken, axed, / run amuck across the yard."

Together with the humor there is sadness—the dead father in "Train Whistle" "tops off soot black trees." Like Plath, one suspects Orsini interpreted her father's death as a rejection. In her *Drawing of a Frog, Grasshopper,* and *Woman in Bed,* the script reads, in part, "each slight, each rejection leaves me wanting a friend." This is raw emotion, like Plath's "Daddy, daddy, you bastard, I'm through."

Orsini's is a fine sensibility—one who knows when dinner is "tired," one who laments having read only one volume of Proust, one who notices "The feathered sheen of milkweed pods." The poet gives as much care to her language as the painter does to her colors. One admires "the periscopic eyes of an alligator" and the description of a bird-song: "hard, sweet notes / fell like apples from the highest boughs . . . a song full, an orchard, spilling." One sees a seascape anew when she says, "The noon sun chips at the sea with an axe" and when the white wings of gulls "heel like a sail / bracing a wall of thin air." Elsewhere she strips words to their roots, as in "dis-ease," giving us both disease and the lack of comfort.

Among the poems I most admire is "Wolf Moon," an unsentimental elegy for an admirable man, the language spare and at war with the subject, which could have been sticky ("he hated / how the winter dark closed in / like a pack of wolves at five"). The poem recalls John Crowe Ransom's aversion to sentiment, as in his own elegy, "Here Lies a Lady":

> Here lies a lady of beauty and high degree,
> Of chills and fever she died, of fever and chills
> The delight of her husband, an aunt, an infant of three,
> And medicos marveling sweetly on her ills . . .

Orsini has chosen an apt title for her book, *An Imperfect Lover,* because the world of any such intense imagination contains much imperfection—imperfect family life, in which affection is withheld; imperfect relationships; imperfect health. Yet creativity has been the vehicle for rescue to a more perfect vision, like the arrival of the great golden ship which is the book's final picture. Orsini's talent is the ability to say a profound thing in a very simple way.

— Robert Phillips
John & Rebecca Moores Professor
University of Houston

AN IMPERFECT LOVER

Poems and Watercolors by Georgianna Orsini

The Heart Makes a Will

My heart lies in wait for me,
crouched inside its leafy lair,
springing forth in puma leaps,
too fast to catch or tame.
Yet, it's not an animal or bird,
and no morning glory, since
it hasn't perished before noon.

Part predator, it watches me,
although it has no eyes,
the insect smarts to inch
its millipedal crawl
across the polar antipodes, or
know how not to freeze at each volcanic blast
that spews its lava expletives
over moments turned to stone.

Once it stopped in front of me
and blindly stared.
I tried to look away and saw
a heart was all I was, in love.
It stayed outside, a silly thing,
much like a chicken, axed,
run amuck across the yard.

All along what made me think
that I could think without a head,
especially with my innards
strewn about, my heart
among the slippery victuals?

Resilient though, it started
up again, for what I couldn't say.

But there it was, not quite the same?
somewhere else, beyond, above,
with added reach and touch,
I thought.

My head back on,
my heart was there
to do with what I wished.
I looked around. "Ha, ha,"
it said. "Where do you suppose
I live? You're still with him?"
I was appalled.

Without a forwarding address,
it had followed any news of him,
living off what had been,
listening for a stealthy way he spoke
intent as any Iroquois tracking game
inside an Adirondack wood,
his manic glee, at capturing
every part I missed.

"No, no," it balked, when I asked it
to come home. Logic, fun and bribes
were tried. And art.
"I'm not a hypocrite" it said,
a little cross at such pretense.
As a heart I thought it might relent,
but no, irate, it had to ask:
"Did I ever lie?"

Heart of Romance

I have a heart of a stone.
When the homeless put out a hand
and invoke Jesus, I walk past:
no emotion outside,
though I lower my eyes.

I have the heart of a nail.
If hurt, I hit back with a word.
With each hammered one,
an echo reports how far I went in,
how close to the pith.

I have the heart of an orphan
hoping for parents
who will take care of me.
Meantime, I invent my own play,
saved by a prince who sweeps me away.

I have the heart of a star,
hounded by fans who flash me
with warm underwear. From behind
dark glasses in my stretch limousine,
I stick out my celluloid tongue.

I have the heart of a lilac.
Without even hearing his voice
I know the perfect lover
calls on the phone, and I break off
one night-scented spring
as long as it rings.

I have the heart of a cow, hock–high
on my country estate, savoring grass.
Social occasions I stand off
with an immovable stare
and a few dumb words; as for company,
I am singled out by my own.

I have the heart of an owl
never let up in my search for who am I,
who are you, follow the usual tracks;
then with large silent wings
happen on things only I see in the dark.

I have the heart of a lover
worked with use and misuse:
the enlargements it gained from loving
equal the spaces no one could fill.
Without warning it rushes into the street
not looking both ways, to follow what it adores.

Parts of Speech

for Bob Phillips

Don't bring me flowers, send me words
uncorked from thin-necked bottles
the wind spins in vertiginous waves.
Sometimes even a sigh will do
from the old dog heaving the three turns
it takes to make its bed; or the sheeps' swollen
stare from the pasture, their noisy tap dance
on the hollow trough, as they stumble
over a succulent call to supper.

Better than a string of pearls,
let me clasp those words;
so suave and blonde, they saunter
through the stands in polo coats
as smooth as sherry sipped from glasses
etched with hunters' whips and cornered beasts.

Not that I can't devour a bestial grunt
or groan, the brunt of stout four-letter
words, if that's what meets a human need.
But bring me words hammered out
from all the rest, faint at first, but grasped
alive, honking from an autumn sky, opening up
the line for me to climb; strong enough
to look straight into the starry sun—
and the speech I'm looking for.

.

Teaching a Female to Sing

"Five dollars for the males who sing,
three for the females," Sam said.
Three was all my allowance could stand.
"I'll teach the female to sing," I assured
my father. Chee Chee, I called her, treated her
with lemony chickweed he showed me
under the humid fir by the back door.
"Come on, chee Chee. Cheep, Cheep."

On the porch below my window
my father relaxed with a highball
and my mother after the office.
He-she, their murmured conversation
echoed the chickadee, nuthatch phrases
punctuating the woods.
"Chee, Chee" they heard the lesson start.
The bird would respond with a willing peep.
It did not sing. "Cheep, cheep," I tried again.

Until one day, without prompting, hard, sweet notes
fell like apples from the highest boughs. I gathered
a song full, an orchard spilling over with my find.
"She sings, she sings," I cried out to my father,
running to tell. "Did you hear? I told you
she'd sing!" My father grinned, underscoring
my wonder, not so surprised he sang.

Train Whistle

That wailing pulls the distance north and south,
shudders over a cinder bed, wakes a household
with a blast. Once this railroad laid down
a countryside, now reclaimed by vines and briars.
Lights at the crossroads shift like red hot coals
as over and over the whistle clears the tracks.
Reservoirs are shed like dragon tails, a half, a third,
an eighth stranded in the sunset's glow. Two swans
look up from the dark as the whistle shrieks,
then swim on in a collaborative peace.

Inside the train, the windows guillotine the tops off
soot black trees. . . without an April leaf to quiver
in the sideswiped air. . . swamp saplings thin as organ
pipes. . . the whistle presses every stop. Lights on,
my face in the glass before a scrim of buildings, poles.
The whistle plays out, the same lullaby notes
heard as a child in the night, from trains that took
my father off, and brought him back. A station stop,
Valhalla called, home of the gods. But my father is dead,
though the whistle persists, returning a home,
where I didn't know I was safe.

Cold Coming On

Hot, hotter under the covers
as the heat wears out, cicadas
at a pitch searching out
every night crevice,
like a bare light bulb
blinding all with its din.

Whatever I mind
shows up again,
each slight, each rejection
leaves me
wanting a friend.
I can't play the piano;
dinner was tired; to live
any better, I haven't read
more than one volume of Proust.

Hear, hear, solicit the insects
not once letting up.
Whatever the effort,
reach out for more.
Persistent, insistent
each unvaried quest
climbs over another
for a chance to be heard.

Comes a cold night,
one lower degree,
it is silent.
Not one exception
in a world losing patience,
I am trying my best.

Canoeing on Tarpon Bay

for Sarah Schilling

No land to walk at all, just trunks with tentacles
that could reach hell, if that was bottom.
Rounded knobs on a slightly sunken log
betray with symmetry the periscopic eyes
of an alligator, cued to drown
a glass-stemmed heron set
to fish at the next river bend.

Water breaks into separate slides, long enough
to film a second sky, trees, legs.
A splash posts some boundary crossed;
even a word tips over a companionable quiet,
shrieking, as water crumples
underneath the thrashing wings.

Almost too weighed down to fly,
the bird discards its mirrored twin.
Violated by a red canoe
with its two paddlers
who trespass one another,
even resting.

Losses

Some never recover
from a slight, a loss;
if you were dead
I'm one of them.

In spite of losing your temper today
at the mutinous minutes you counted
to an hour I took, taking in too much
of the store for you to endure my promise:
"It shouldn't take long." Lost,

minutes at night when we wake
at the same time. In the quiet you hand
me water thinking it's what I need.
Or, once back to sleep, if I touch
your hand, it remembers to take mine.

Some never recover
from a slight, a loss;
if you were dead
I'm one of them.

Closing a Door

. . . silence kept house,
took all your praise
to pretty my walls,
papering over my faults.

Without knocking, silence
broke in, found its tongue
slipped from the mouth
to the root cellar of sex.

That long ago mushrooms:
time spent underground
whitens the flesh
kept from the light.

Not even once
have I called out your name
from a silence so loud:
O love, I never can say.

Love Becomes Us

"They won't last," they said,
knowing our unvoiced differences,
sure your fickle reputation
and my more rooted past
would clash.

Made for this mystery,
how far love goes,
past time and effort-
less tears, to find just us
was what we wanted most.

Such knowledge was never carried
by angels with lilies
from heaven, all light
and feathered visitation,
but sighted
in the slower workings
round our day-to-day talk and lives,
with their lonesome limitations

that come to a full stop
surprised how generous
we've become, spilling over
like the leaves this fall,
looking out to see
the close-to tedious green
turn gold and red.

Putting aside all else
you open the door
and call out
"Where are you?"
"Here," I have to answer.

In Concert

Hidden away in the music
you found my hand. I might have been
the prettiest there in a dress I'd sewed.
I felt sure of you, further complimented
by the zucca and rice you'd cooked for supper.
So many times I found myself counting on you
to catch the forgotten milk on the stove,
to balance the books my arithmetic failed.

At intermission you reached the lobby
ahead of me, where you spotted
a young girl you hardly knew.
Pretty enough to caress her cheek
with your hand. "It's just my way,"
you said, when I wondered out loud,
with a self ripped out, hideous, inert,
even knowing a week ago
I touched the cheek of another
with the same careless affection.

The Value of Nice

How the noon sun chips
at the sea with an axe,
stacking the shade under the pines.
White gulls sharpen their wings
to a point and pass. There are words
as acute. "Darling" you won't say,
although I may hold the sound
of your sweet voice to my ear;
note you do not insist
or even wish to be found.

I hover over words.
But I am not what you are looking for,
just someone you will speak of as "nice,"
perhaps "dear." So when I tell you
about the gulls, it will not be important
how the white wings heel like a sail
bracing a wall of thin air.

The Perfect Lover

*Now I'm shivering so violently that the tree is not only sway-
ing but vibrating. But I am concerned about becoming stiff
from the cold and too weak to hold with one hand and take
notes with the other. But I'm determined to stay because the
ravens have come.*

— Bernd Heinrich
from *Ravens in Winter*

She won't have to be anyone, or do anything at all.
Just be there to receive the man
who studied ravens four cold winters.
No need for her to prepare a meal,
or light a fire; her fascination will be
without the least accomplishment.
She will be the woman in the window
uncovering a snowflake's fall,
each more visible than the last,
fluffing up the down for beds
where bears will seek their snug oblivions;
while ravens circle over the sheep carcasses
he carted at midnight through the crusted drifts,
then back down to thaw, then up again to tempt
what only he had guessed was so worthwhile.
All day he watched with eyes locked
into the frozen sky, in case he missed
the one dark speck from which
he could exclaim what ravens are.
As she wishes to be studied by that scholar's eye.

A Hypocritic Oath

There was a recipe for mice
in the July *Gourmet*,
touted as different,
delicious to try. Why?
A list of ingredients
caught my eye.
Not on the market
but a snap to catch,
I raided a nest,
squirming and fresh,
kept in the cabinet
under the sink.
Ripe as cheese,
no longer pink, but aged
by a tincture of fur;
their shiny eyes
threaded like seeds
seemed to swivel,
without an iris
to look at me.

Plump and juicy,
they thrived exclusively
on mother's milk,
thus qualified for plum de mouse;
but being alive,
the trouble was
how would they die?
Weren't the same skills
applied to lobsters of use?
Such as: bring a pot of hot water
to boil; drop in.

Maybe a tendon to clip,
or target to hit at the base of the skull,
conjuring up an instant kill.

Nothing was said
as I attentively read
to set the oven at 350 degrees,
slow enough
for a cookie dough.
The brood was spooned
on an aluminum sheet,
one here, one there
in shapely rows of batter.
But reviewing such runny material,
would there be enough room?
What if it started to crawl
every which way in the heat
and ended up congealed
in a sticky heap?

I lightly salted
the squirming flesh,
peppered the noses
able to sniff, but not enough
to scent a threat.
I did it, I did it—
shut the oven, set the timer,
held my breath
(it was as easy as that),
my guests were due
when the entrée was through.

Eight minutes later,
just the right amount for fish,
but was it too much

for a tender dish?
I opened the oven—
Plump and Juicy
were done too crisp.

Would I call it a disaster
or treat it as a blackened
Cajun feast, upgrade it
to a French *souris*?

I polished my words
to a silver shine,
inviting my guests
to please sit down,
and not wait upon
their hostess to start.
The candles were lit,
an icy swan at the center
dripped, as each one
lifted a fork with a slice
still shaped like a tiny mouse.

Which brought out talk
sparkling from vintage hyperbole,
in some disrepute with
any regard for the truth:
"Oh Marjorie Lois, you make us swear,
it just isn't fair
you'd be the one
with the aplomb
to undertake such a cunning roast—
(what's its name, almost there
on the tip of the tongue?)

And so well executed,
was it reviewed in *Cooking Lite*,
or renowned in the Michelin Guide?
Now we won't fuss over
finding such exotic ingredients,
or travel so far,
seeing Paris put down
by the dish in front of us."

A Complaint

Give her an F in fellatio,
the soprano's falsetto,
a cover-up
for a failure
to fuck.

Far from the heart,
she was given to watch
porno flicks in the dark.
Its stars pointed out
how to lick each private part.

Like a drill sergeant
the tongue's lashings
marched down,
then up and around
the raw pricks,
till they foamed
in a pivotal moan.
That's no lollypop
sucked in the mouth.
The semen may pop,
but what a to-do
when the juice
sticks like glue.

As for its spice
to the sexual act,
it's a deviant device
compared to the shared
thrust in the cunt
that unearths
the mind's elements,
where a woman's assent
loosens its hold
on enough pleasure for both.

Worm Moon

You never age.
You were all my love,
which means I don't dare ask
how you are when I see you.
Nor do you need to, even,
given a worm's underground
means of measuring
the least sexual tremor.
It's not likely I will ever be able
to tunnel through that darkness
to hear you merely say hello.

I thought I had gone somewhere
else, yet I'm seated opposite you
in the kind of restaurant we liked,
where the food was cheap,
the owner favored us.
We don't say much, every mouthful
revered like the frothy green tea
whisked in a Japanese ceremony,
exquisitely erotic.

A word would end us up in bed.
A flower, too.
A peony once stood in a glass by my pillow,
a white *festiva maxima*
flecked with red from the heart,
before it shattered.
Is that why I don't ask
how you could have left,
about the other women
studied like religious texts

you would illuminate?
I look at the full moon
and note I still have time
before I'm jealous.

·

Green Corn Moon

A crow's beak on a roadkill,
you feast on my vitals.
All the while I'm not dead
to the fact you're unhappy.
I'm not the cause,
just the passer-by who waits
for a severe moon to hit you
like highlights stunning the night traffic.

In that lunar land, cold enough
to give all earth a heated argument,
to withhold a summer's green,
I should know emotions
run the course of seasons,
plunder any stored provisions.

So used, how can we fit in
to August cornfields
seeding the frantic mice
at home beneath the crafted stalks?
What force can stay the fecund crop
about to split each tassel top,
and harvest it before the kernels
spoil?   Can I

gather up past ritual
and plunge the ears
into the killing salted water
to boil seven minutes,

drain and slather them with butter,
taking a chance you love me too,
and will not call corn alien
and refuse to eat?

Snow Moon

Almost a year since he wanted me
to know: "There's a rainbow out back."
Unexpected, a summer sight in winter
although it is his height, stooped
in the average doorway, that stops me still.
Neither husband nor lover, with their planted fields
of promised life and ponds whose thin ice
is never marked DANGER, he approached
more safely, as friend; no one I had to bother with,
though I did. Brighter, straighter, I was flattered
to feel as smart and good.

Wakeful this night, I see the moon feathered
with the sheen of milkweed pods.
Ice in the air sharpens that death I want to stop.
I put on the light to read what he'd read
from Trollope. It is the resonant sound
of his voice: what he would note, or add
with wit. I mark him, like important passages,
close with the book. *Nota bene:*
the unprinted end pages, blank as the moon,
not one star shows in a sky . . . not thinking of him,
but of snow.

Wolf Moon

for Jack Brown, 1934–1993

Alone, he hated
how the winter dark closed in
like a pack of wolves at five.
Other people fitted into herds
or flocks. He stuck out.
A human prey, each wolf hair
stiffened, the glassy eyes
sharp as sleet, waiting
for some sign he could not keep up.

That week the tepid sun
melted snow that crusted at night;
the death paws would lope across
without a print. Ignorant of the spring seed
sprouting on his porch, or that he loved
someone, or of the time he needed to paint
the intricacies of rocks and lichen.
"My closest friend" some said.
He did not bore or brag. That he knew
more than most, careful to knock
before breaking into another's thought

was not enough to spare him.
From the hollows of their lore,
wolves hungered for that good,
the way marked vulnerable.
The winter air was enough to tear his flesh,
but the killing stroke was clearly professional;

he never woke to fear a predator.
That howling chiseled on a knoll would outlast
a date and name on weather-beaten stone,
the twelfth, when the moon began to fail.

Frances Melissa Nanny

Once I saw her hair undone.
I was enthralled as though
I'd seen a nest of garter snakes,
start up every witch way. My nanny,
called Grandmother: usually, her hair
was wound in a bun, its cushion
tufted with platinum pins, her mouth
pulled in, still holding them.

Most of her words stayed stored
like the Belgian lace tablecloth
layered in tissue paper, unwrapped
for Sundays, Easter, and Christmas
occasions as when, washing my hands
with the big cake of sandalwood
soap, swished back and forth
in the apricot basin's sudsy water,
"Here, honeybunch," she said,
wiping my hands on a starched
tea towel. An unexpected sweet
hoarded long in a family hard–
pressed to say their love out loud.

Even the Best Men

Just that once he slapped me.
Wheeled from the front to punctuate
my adolescent blubbering in the back.
I was failing algebra, the tutor too.

On a usual day, a piper to follow,
singing as he did the usual chores.
"All aboard that's going aboard,"
he conducted his children awake
school mornings, collecting the dogs
as he led them all. Missed the weeks

he traveled, as head of sales
for Ludlum Steel, to Birmingham
where they rolled the molten iron,
Cleveland, where they soldered planes.
Sunday nights, before the sleeper train,
he climbed the shoe stand in the station
where Jimmy shined his size 13 shoes:
two parallel giant apricot tongues.
Beside him in the other chairs, our
Buster Browns treated to a polish too.

Travel only lured him home,
moving no further than his coops,
stocking the chickens and pheasants
with fresh water and feed, pruning
the old apple trees before lunch;
then a game of cards before the fire
with Uncle Jack or Uncle Ted,
Mother knitting socks on the sofa.

But not that Saturday he picked me
up from the lesson.
I had never been hit. Slapped.
The sting, for a second, with its leveling
act between grown-up and child.
At impact, a harder severance.

Tomato Sandwiches

At the last moment it rained.
Though underage, we were allowed
to drive the station wagon into the overgrown
pasture. We stopped in the ferny asparagus bed
gone to seed. Rain tap-danced on the roof!
Across the windshield the wipers pulled
the water like curtains on a puppet show,
tucking us in.

Three sisters, we dined formally to start,
unwrapping the wax paper sheets, guided
by their neat hospital corners and folds.
But biting into the pillowy white bread
the mayonnaise oozed, and the lettuce
slipped away like hair tied with silk ribbon.
Next, the tomatoes squished and slid,
spattering our faces, our laps, the seats.
We were silly, then sillier as we pointed out
the boring carrot and celery sticks, the dull
boiled eggs, whose shells we resoundingly
cracked on our heads, laughing hard enough
we had to hold our sides. It hurt.

Chronic competitors, made wary for life
in the arms of parental approval, where else
would we find a checkpoint so lax, waving us
through to someone as close as a sister?

How I Came to Build the Bomb

Nothing remiss with my heritage,
my parents believed
in children and dogs.
I started to go wrong
with a baby sister:
"Get rid of her," I implied.

How I cried out for my mother.
What was she doing downstairs?
On and on till the tears were dry,
before she came to my crib.
Then we prayed to a God
I was supposed to obey.

Sent to camp, I was homesick
couldn't adjust to so many goals,
though I got the good sportsmanship
right—Lie! What a cheerful,
cooperative camper I became,
awarded two silver stars.

From then on I chose a life
of my own. Except I married
too soon, an honest, kind,
a marvelous man, though a bit
restrained. Trouble was
he never made love.

Set up for an affair,
it only took the soft,
emollient voice of a Syrian sheik
to run off, where I joined

a stable of women he rode
for his pleasure alone.

With reason I turned
to a wandering Jew.
Now that one I loved.
My hold on him was my soul.
But, a traveling man, love
was a burden he couldn't take on.

Once he left, I got serious;
I was destroyed.
Took all his letters, gifts,
what he'd said
as major components,
started in on the bomb.

To which I added
a second marriage,
just like the manual said.
Knew I'd gotten it right,
just to hear his bad temper
set off a blast.

What a racket,
what a sight,
my whole world exploded.
I blew up with the rest.
Stunned, my fragments
littered the ground.

Though I pleaded an innocence,
I was arrested for my part
in the plot, sentenced
to a life of hard labor.

If I wanted to come out,
I had to act right in the head.

Cut off from temptation
my behavior improved.
I served the minimum time
to put back an ear,
an eye; it took longer
to bypass the heart.

When I came out
I was rehabilitated,
wanted no part of a bomb
made out of too many parts
that exploded, ruined
the look on my face.

I started halfway—
in the house, made the bed,
made dinner, a garden,
gradually a book,
and a marriage that got better
rather than worse.

Looking around,
I was attached to a home,
a stretch of contentment,
even in winter, as pleased
when the sun sneaked its fires
through the paralyzed trees.

As simple as goldfish
hearing my steps,
bubbling in luminous schools

at the top of the pond to be fed.
Far from the wrath that set off a bomb,
those fires blackening
too much of the sky.

Orchestra Conductor

She could have died from a burst appendix
at six, or later, her first kiss, or later,
a life later, from the lack of one.
But at six, in a blue satin cape, its red flare
at the collar to show conductor status,
she stepped before the first grade:
Patsy Kelly, Clara Kabowski, Patsy Ganser,
Diane Ziegler, Sammy Bowen, Doris Smith,
Mary Katchuturian, Russell Gritch, Jackie Cummings,
Gibby Golden, cross-eyed Betty, and Donny Hayden,
who fought with Jackie to place his rug
next to Patsy's black curls at nap time.

Back to the audience, she raised her baton,
pointed to the solo triangles, sticks, drums,
sandpaper blocks, bells, sounded together
when she waved both arms, while the "March
of the Wooden Soldiers" circled the wound-up Victrola
Miss Dietrich worked in the wings. For the first time—
applause, singled out, a bow back.

Next day: "It hurts here." Doctors fingered
her rectum. "That's not where." The lifted importance
as her father carried her towards an appendectomy,
wrapped in her parents' attar of rose wool blanket,
its corner tag with the curly horned sheep
ready to jump off a cliff. Down the hospital's
marble vacancies, her mother's tiptoe near,

her life might have ended under the vertigo
plunge of the ether. Yet lives are made
on less than a moment's notice, its acclaim,
and a participative bow back.

Literary Lion

Seagulls pried the day alive,
started small brush fires in the goldenrod.
On the path a rabbit stood up
like I'd come into its room.
Good morning enough, but I went a ways
to visit the island's writer in residence.

She came from the garden
with a bowl of grapes, her hair in tendrils
as befitted the vines. "Making jelly?" I asked.
Nodding her head, she sat down on the step,
not inviting me in. I handed her a piece
of Caprese cake, its sugar slumped under its wrap.
She took it like I'd given her a task;
I wanted it back.

"What an irresistible sight," I ventured,
shy to expound on the sweeping water before us,
the charm of her old clapboard house.
"Oh, yes…" I then asked about mutual friends.
"She's the same, but I don't know how…."
"Donald?" "He's slower after the stroke."
"How do you mean?" " Just slower."
"I guess you heard about the fire."
She slumped on the step to a whispered "Yes."

Unbidden, I didn't sit in one of three empty chairs.
But quick as a subject exiting a queen,
I withdrew to an island aerie. The moors
and sea and sky resumed their places
like disturbed animals continuing
to graze after a killing has passed.

My Friend

for Ruth Phinney Stevens

Having a friend means
not to be singled out by a sky
overturned, its color drained into the sea;
by distances that never catch up to the land,
not fastened down by a tree.

Just to think we will meet
for steamed mussels today
(and tomorrow the pork tenderloin
sweetened with prunes,
we planned back at the market,
centers me in new hospitality).

Provisions of seagulls, seaweed and sand.
Books and talk to open
like the clams we dig,
a walk planted with late flowers,
strung on the keening seagulls
pinned against the wind.

For our table I will pick the ghost dandelion
she mistakes for a June buttercup.
I am not about to correct, pampered
by an ease, knowing, and not knowing
the transience of friends,
of no consequence to the sea.

Downdraft

Despite a screen on the window,
the damper closed, a bat slips
down a chimney flue. Blind, it reads
the sleeping room, lulled by sunnier
sights, then swerves, wings flap
like untrimmed sails coming about.
Whatever you loathe, whatever you fear
snags on that erratic flight,
desperate to find a place to hide.

Like a sliver of ice it fits a crack,
that widens to a scream at something
other than a mouse with wings.
Aerialist of the parabola, each downswing
grazes creature lore, trapped inside
snarled-up hair; until someone sane
opens a door to the cool night air,
vacuums the room, smoothes
the trampled sheets, turns off the light,
then on, face to face with that creature
folded up within, creeping upside down,
inert.

City Island

Gulls commute whole hemispheres,
their lurching cries
speeding to a metropolitan screech
as their talons grasp a struggling fish.
Leaves populate the brush
where apprehensive rabbits
wait for dark, form clumps
where beach plum ripens
its glistening jam,
where winds rule head high
the bludgeoned oak and pine,
and poison ivy breathes
infection on a deviant step.

People appear no nearer
than those from a high rise
looking down. Populated
by the late-day cries of children
coming home, mimicking seagull
exclamations over scavenged finds,
is a place to take what people harm, dis-
ease condemned by a landscape
so open, that a heart's mind comes out
of hiding, like one of the rabbits
sensing it's clear.

Yoga Lesson

Out of the flute a golden ship appears,
square-rigged sails mapping the golden sky.
No wind or wake as it crosses a becalmed
ocean, majestic, glorious, non-sensual.
There is no stopping its course;
there is no one to stop.
Just a ship carved out of wooden notes,
the chanted bells softening all danger.
Then it goes behind an island's cliff
that plays with birds no longer there.
A lighter boat soon follows:
its golden sails list with summer light.
Agitated, livelier, there are waves now.
Female, she dances nearer and nearer
to a sense of loss—she wants him back.
The flute is bolder now, the bells shaken.

Out on the street a siren identifies
the rescue squad on exactly the same pitch
as the plaintive song. It centers on an emergency:
speeded engines, wheels,
rushed to some stricken helplessness.
The moment reworks a room, a tree
reaps golden leaves outside the window,
a creak peoples the wooden stairs.
I want to meet my teacher's father
come for a visit. She tells us to focus on
four cleansing breaths. Leads us into relaxation.
I am not deluded. I see my happiness.
Close enough to remember the time
you reached for my hand.

Georgianna Orsini, Outsider Artist

Just under the undulating surface of the name Georgianna Orsini stands the backbone of her girlhood name: Georgianna Coolidge Sherman. The transformation of Annie, as she was called at home, into Georgie, as she was known at school and camp, then into Anne as a young woman, and finally into Georgianna Orsini is a love story, and that is the subject both of her poetry and her paintings. It is a complex story—an "imperfect" one, the sort that entices because its path is not clear but disappears into shadow, reappearing again. Annie Sherman was born on May 11, 1932, in Albany, New York, to a family with New England roots, and grew up as the third of four children, three girls and a boy. She had a childhood full of dancing classes and smocked dresses, one that gave her plenty of dreamtime. She was the sort of girl who climbed down from her limb in an apple tree with a brand-new idea and corralled her little sister into staging whatever fantasy had seized her. She loved the Emma Willard School and made lifelong friends there. Two of her best friends have known her nearly seventy years.

These friends recognized early, as did her family, and later her beaus, her husbands, and reporters for *Women's Wear Daily* and *House & Garden*, that they were in contact with a unique nature, bursting with talents and enthusiasms but with no apparent need to put the products of those enthusiasms out in the world. She painted, she played the piano and composed music, she wrote poetry. A superficial eye might might misperceive her as a dilettante. But a closely regarding eye might detect a private genius. She would be the first person to pooh-pooh the idea that strictures of her class or sex had anything to do with what someone with a brand new MFA degree might call her lack of professionalism. One might say that her ambition drove her to her own interior, a vibrant, inner world with a small, immediate circle of friends as her audience.

Anne Sherman was possessed of sublime domestic talents that began to flower even before she became Georgianna Orsini. She is a discerning but whimsical cook, a distinguished but fantastical gardener (featured in *The American Woman's Garden*), a designer and seamstress of her own clothes, a maker of her own jewelry, and a keeper of an animal menagerie of dogs, cats, exotic birds, doves, canaries, and even at one time Jacob's sheep—for mowing the lawn. Realizing her fantasies has been her life's work, although work is not a word one associates with Georgianna Orsini, however many hours she might devote to a task. Her arts are a product of sheer energy that, while it takes time, seems to exist outside of time—or perhaps is lost in it.

In this she shares the qualities of Outsider Artists. In the strictest sense Art Brut (Raw Art), as the French painter Jean Dubuffet defined it in 1948, was reserved for psychiatric patients and completely untrained artists, all of whom had no sense that they were visual artists at all. But as the kernel of Art Brut flowered into the North American concept of Outsider Art, leading to galleries, organizations, and websites devoted to arguing over what art in the raw state actually is, an idea of an extremely inventive, formally untrained artist working outside conventions but aware of those conventions began to emerge. Orsini is this sort of artist.

And are there Outsider Poets as well? I don't mean bitter poets heckling tastemakers from the sidelines, but poets not traditionally trained in the MFA system, unconnected to any group of poets with a distinct aesthetic, aware of contemporary poetry, aware of poetic traditions, but unattached to ideas of poetry as they are hammered from teacher to student, one generation of poets to the next? A poet creating in a cave, so to speak? Georgianna Orsini—educated, but untrained— falls into that category, too.

Outside of the academy, outside of the world of letters, outside of a gallery system, her idea of ambition has been to conjure up a world of memory for her paintings and an overlapping world of emotions for her poems, each illustrating the other (the poems illustrating paintings as well as the other way around), and her idea of study is tutelage. She has taken private piano, drawing and painting lessons for seven decades, and has been an avid reader of the English and American canon of poetry since childhood. Her work, while disciplined, is free. If she weren't so sophisticated in her perceptions, one might be tempted to class her watercolors and some of her poems as naïf. Orsini has the impulse of a William Blake but not his scope or obsession. Robert Phillips compares her to Beatrix

Potter. Her work also recalls the British naturalist and watercolorist Edith Holden (whose 1906 illustrated diary, full of observations, quotations from poetry, and vivid botanical and avian illustrations, was published in a facsimile edition in 1977 as *The Country Diary of an Edwardian Lady*).

But judging by the sharp vocabulary of her poetry, one could hardly call Georgianna Orsini lady-like. After a stint at Wellesley College and a brief, early marriage, she arrived in Greenwich Village with a bicycle, a sheaf of poems, a watercolor pad and a job at Columbia University's International House. It was the 1950s, and between events at International House, her friend the actor Roscoe Lee Brown took her up to Steepletop to meet Norma Millay, Edna St. Vincent Millay's sister. And Leonard Cohen took her camping in the Laurentian Mountains, their traveling companions Cohen's Canadian compatriot the poet Irving Layton and his then wife Aviva.

After she and Cohen parted ways, Roscoe Lee Brown brought Anne to one of the first truly sophisticated Italian restaurants in New York. It was the era when Marlon Brando played Stanley Kowalski in *A Streetcar Named Desire* on Broadway and on film, and Elizabeth Taylor starred as Maggie in the film version of *Cat on a Hot Tin Roof*. In New York a cup of coffee came in a thick china cup from Chock Full O' Nuts or the Automat. But Armando Orsini, after life-or-death escapades eluding both Fascists and Nazis in Italy at the end of World War II, had come to New York, first as the lover of the fabled stripper Lily St. Cyr, and then to strike out on his own, joining with his brother to give Midtown one of its first tastes of espresso. Late at night Brando and Taylor and an increasing gaggle of celebrities from Grace Kelly to Lauren Bacall came for the silky pastas and sharp espresso. The restaurant was called Orsini's, and circulating nightly among the tables was Armando Orsini, suave and lanky, a Rossano Brazzi-type who spent his after-hours at El Morocco and The Stork Club.

Still sensuous and sophisticated at nearly eighty, Orsini can tell you of his first glimpse of his future wife at the table with Roscoe Lee Brown. They were quoting poems to one another. Surrounded by glamour that needed his presence as an audience to thrive, Armando Orsini sat down with a woman who carried her world with her, seeming never to need an audience. She was not an ornament. She possessed a fabled set of inner resources, modeled after those heroines of the nineteenth-century novels she loved to read and talk about. Tall, dark-haired, and straight of posture, she wore a dress she had made herself—not out of necessity but playfulness. And so a forty-year love affair and marriage began.

"Let's play a game," Georgianna once said to me. "If you were a man, who would you be?" she asked, but before I could even think, she burst out with her own answer. "I'd be Armando. There's no one whose courage and bravery and honesty I admire more."

After their honeymoon skiing in the Dolomites, they went on to Rome to meet Armando's mother, the widow of a sea captain. On return trips they ventured further into the still agrarian Italian landscape and restored a Tuscan farm which they made a home. Armando would alternate two weeks with his brother in the New York restaurant and two weeks with his wife in Tuscany. There, cooking, drawing, writing, gardening, learning Italian and waiting for Armando to burst in the door, Anne reclaimed all the syllables of the name she was born with: Georgianna. She was still creating her fantasy worlds of flowers and animals, but now she had grown into her birth name, its syllables tumbling into her husband's world, his language, where it seemed her name rightfully belonged. In the circular way identities have of achieving themselves, she had come around to her origins and found at last what she would call herself. Another way to put it is that she found her calling—or, what others should call her. And she had located her world, one of beauty and splendid isolation, with a vibrant wire to the world of glitter, her husband, Armando. When she was in New York with Armando, *Women's Wear Daily* tracked her self-designed outfits. But when she was home in Italy, she rested in the lap of her own imagination.

Eventually the Orsinis returned to North America, living in Pawling, New York; Vermont; and New York City; and later retiring to Sanibel Island, Florida; and Cashiers, North Carolina. Georgianna Orsini has led anything but an overspecialized life, another reason to call her both an Outsider Artist and an Outsider Poet.

Yet she has a conviction peculiar to specialists: that to live meaningfully requires a close and careful examination of the world. She cultivates the habits of a naturalist in her watercolors and poems. Her birds and flowers are casually yet precisely alive, as in Edith Holden's diary, but also as in the offhand, intimate vividness of the nineteenth-century British Romantic poet John Clare. Orsini has something of Clare's naturalist eye, a sympathy with animals and certainly an intimacy with flora. Right now, whether among her Sanibel lemon trees or on her mountaintop in Cashiers, she writes and paints accompanied by a pug, a rottweiler, a Persian cat, an Amazon grey parrot, a roseate cockatoo, and a dozen canaries at her side—not to mention her ebullient husband.

Unobsessed with line breaks, never in her life having used "work-shop" as a verb, creating musical and psychological rhythms in her poetry that allow each image to spin in a vortex of feeling, Orsini composes poems about emotional states that are so palpable they are nearly tactile. Entirely witty and wise as a grown-up companion, she still inhabits that girlhood world of her imagination. She and I first met in 1989 at the Croton Public Library in Westchester when Robert Phillips, who hosted a library poetry reading series in which I was a guest, introduced us. The next weekend Georgianna invited me and my companion to her house, Cloudy Woods, in Pawling, New York. It was approaching Halloween. The house was reached by a long drive through dense woods. Just as we rounded a curve I saw an entire cardboard cemetery. Our front tires must have tripped a switch, because lights sprang on and ghosts on guy wires flew out at us. The house was too far away from the road for anyone but Georgianna and Armando and their guests to see it. Her effort was made not for the public, however, but to tickle that inner world of fancy that she—and I—are convinced is the source of personal happiness.

— Molly Peacock
Toronto

A Portfolio of Watercolors

The Heart Makes a Will

"My heart lies in wait for me"

Heart of Romance

"Without warning it rushes into the street
not looking both ways, to follow what it adores."

Teaching a Female to Sing

"He-she, their murmured conversation
echoed the chickadee-nuthatch phrases"

Cold Coming On

"... in a world losing patience,
I am trying my best"

Canoeing on Tarpon Bay

"A splash posts some boundary crossed"

Losses

"Or, once back to sleep, if I touch
your hand, it remembers to take mine."

Closing a Door

"... from a silence so loud:

O love, I never can say"

Love Becomes Us

" . . . how far love goes,
past time and effort–
less tears."

FEMALE (LEFT) COURTS DOMINANT
MALE RAVEN

G.O.

The Perfect Lover

". . . the one dark speck from which
he could exclaim what ravens are."

A Hypocritic Oath

". . . their shiny eyes
threaded like seeds
seemed to swivel
without an iris
to look at me."

Worm Moon

"A word would end us up in bed.
A flower, too."

Green Corn Moon

"What force can stay the fecund crop
about to split each tassel top?"

Wolf Moon

"Alone, he hated
how the winter dark closed in
like a pack of wolves at five."

Frances Melissa Nanny

". . . in a family hard
pressed to say their love out loud."

Even the Best Men

"Just that once he slapped me."

Tomato Sandwiches

"Across the windshield the wipers pulled
the water like curtains on a puppet show,
tucking us in."

How I Came to Build the Bomb

". . . a bomb
made out of too many parts
that exploded, ruined
the look on my face."

Orchestra Conductor

"Patsy Kelly, Clara Kabowski, Patsy Ganser,
Diane Ziegler, Sammy Bowen . . . Russell Gritch"

Literary Lion

"I handed her a piece
of Caprese cake, its sugar slumped under its wrap."

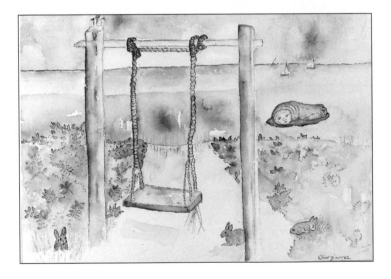

My Friend

". . . a walk planted with late flowers,
strung on the keening seagulls
pinned against the wind."

Within the image: nothing to do but look at a week long shimmer

GIORGIANNA 07

City Island

"...a heart's mind comes out
of hiding, like one of the rabbits
sensing it's clear."

Yoga Lesson

"Just a ship carved out of wooden notes,
the chanted bells softening all danger."